Thank you!

To my mother, Frances Shapiro —LS
To Kyoko Yoshida —HT

It's Time to Start Using Your Words

Thank you, Mama.

a transition times book

Lawrence E. Shapiro, Ph.D.
Illustrated by **Hideko Takahashi**

Instant Help Books

Peter was trying hard to put together a jigsaw puzzle. But no matter how hard he tried, the pieces did not fit.

He threw the puzzle across the room.

"It's time to start using your words," said Peter's mommy.

"When you tell me what's wrong,
then I can help."

Lena dropped a book on her toe and started to cry.

She cried and cried, and then
she cried some more.

"It's time to start using your words," said Lena's daddy.

"If you tell me why you're crying,
I can help make it better."

Andre pointed to food when he wanted to eat . . .

and to his cup when he wanted to drink.

"It's time to start using your words," said Andre's babysitter.

"Tell me what you want to eat,
and I can get it for you."

Sara got a toy bunny from her grandma.

She hugged the bunny, but she didn't say a thing to her grandma.

"It's time to start using your words," said Sara's grandma.

Say "thank you" when
you get a gift.

Use your words when you are happy.

Use your words when you are sad.

My dolly is broken!

Use your words when you are angry.

Use your words when you play with your friends.

Use your words to show how much you care.

This is yummy.
Thank you!

You're the best
grandma in the
whole world.

Advice for Parents

Dear Parents,

Your child's language develops at a very predictable rate. He will say his first word around his first birthday. By age three, he will speak in three-word phrases and ask for what he needs in simple sentences. By age five, your child will hold a conversation pretty much like an adult, using his vocabulary of more than 2,000 words.

It is between the ages of three and four that you should expect your child to start using words to express his feelings. If he is frustrated, hurt, or sad, he should be able to tell you why. He should also be able to use his words in his social interactions, using phrases such as "please," "thank you," and "may I?" with both children and adults.

But language development is not the only thing that determines how well a child verbalizes his thoughts and feelings. The ability to manage emotions comes from a different part of the brain than a child's language development, and these two areas must interact smoothly before a child can express his emotional needs and desires in words. Some children develop the neural connections between these areas later than others, and these children might need extra encouragement to "use their words," particularly when they are upset.

As you probably already know, children who express their feelings in words rather than just act them out are simply easier to parent. As you encourage your young child to use her words, you will find that she is less likely to become frustrated, less prone to tantrums and other expressions of anger, and generally more cooperative.

Communication is also an important part of your child's social development. By the age of three, children start to learn the social skills that will help them make friends, resolve conflicts, and develop lifelong social graces that will define their most important relationships. Children who express both positive and negative feelings in words will usually have an easier time navigating their social world, and the skills that they develop when they are young will likely continue through their childhood, becoming the foundation of their adult social success.

Teaching your child the importance of emotional communication will even have an impact on his academic achievement. Studies have shown that one of the most important factors in school success is the positive attention that teachers give to children. In other words, if your child's teacher likes him, he has an advantage over other children. And teachers universally agree that children who have learned positive communication skills are their classroom favorites.

There are several things that you can do to help your child use his words instead of just acting on his feelings:

1. **Be a good role model. When you calmly express your feelings in words, you show your child exactly how you want him to behave.**

2. Use magazines or picture books to encourage children to talk about their feelings. Find pictures of children and adults with various expressions on their faces and ask your child to say what the person in the picture is thinking or feeling. Then you should do the same.

3. When your child plays with dolls or action figures, join in. Take the role of one of the dolls or figures and, again, be a good role model by describing what you think that character might be thinking or feeling. You can even direct the role-play to mimic events in your child's life, having your character speak in the words that you want your child to use.

For other ideas about how to encourage your child to use his words through play, visit our website, www.TransitionTimesBooks.com.

Good luck!
Lawrence Shapiro, Ph.D.

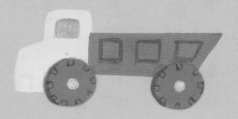

The **transition times** series is designed to help parents understand the importance of addressing developmental issues at the right time and in the right way. Each book addresses a specific transition in the lives of children, when they often need a gentle nudge forward on the road to responsibility and independence. The books provide parents with a way to talk to their children that will hold their interest and make facing life's challenges seem less overwhelming. The books also help parents understand age-appropriate expectations, and give them a simple and clear context to set realistic limits. Reading the books to children will make bumpy transition times just a little bit smoother.

It's Time to Give Up Your Pacifier

Lawrence E. Shapiro, Ph.D.
Illustrated by Hideko Takahashi

It's Time to Sit Still in Your Own Chair

Lawrence E. Shapiro, Ph.D.
Illustrated by Hideko Takahashi

It's Time to Sleep in Your Own Bed

Lawrence E. Shapiro, Ph.D.
Illustrated by Hideko Takahashi

It's Time to Start Using Your Words

Thank you, Mama.

Lawrence E. Shapiro, Ph.D.
Illustrated by Hideko Takahashi